DOMINOES

Lord Arthur Savile's Crime and Other Stories

LEVEL TWO   700 HEADWORDS

OXFORD
UNIVERSITY PRESS

Great Clarendon Street, Oxford OX2 6DP

Oxford University Press is a department of the University of Oxford.
It furthers the University's objective of excellence in research, scholarship,
and education by publishing worldwide in

Oxford New York

Auckland Cape Town Dar es Salaam Hong Kong Karachi
Kuala Lumpur Madrid Melbourne Mexico City Nairobi
New Delhi Shanghai Taipei Toronto

With offices in

Argentina Austria Brazil Chile Czech Republic France Greece
Guatemala Hungary Italy Japan Poland Portugal Singapore
South Korea Switzerland Thailand Turkey Ukraine Vietnam

OXFORD and OXFORD ENGLISH are registered trade marks of
Oxford University Press in the UK and in certain other countries

This edition © Oxford University Press 2010

The moral rights of the author have been asserted

Database right Oxford University Press (maker)

First published in Dominoes 2003

2014 2013 2012 2011 2010

10 9 8 7 6 5 4 3 2 1

ISBN: 978 0 19 424885 3 BOOK
ISBN: 978 0 19 424837 2 BOOK AND MULTIROM PACK
MULTIROM NOT AVAILABLE SEPARATELY

Printed in China

ACKNOWLEDGEMENTS

Illustrations by: David Roberts/Artist Partners

The publisher would like to thank the following for permission to reproduce photographs:

Cover: Getty Images (Going Home at Dusk, 1882/John Atkinson Grimshaw)

Bridgeman Art Library Ltd pp13 (Our Drawing Room at York, Best, Mary Ellen (1809–91) /
Private Collection), 37 (The New Model, 1883 (oil on canvas), Skutezky, Dome or Dominik
(1850–1921) / © Russell-Cotes Art Gallery and Museum, Bournemouth, UK), 42 (Changing
Homes, 1862 (oil on canvas), Hicks, George Elgar (1824–1914) / © Geffrye Museum, London,
UK); Getty Images p61 (Oscar Wilde/W. and D. Downey/Stringer); The Art Archive p49
(L'Américaine carriage, engraving from 1852 series by Monpezat/Musée National de la
voiture et du tourisme Compiègne / Gianni Dagli Orti).

DOMINOES

Series Editors: Bill Bowler and Sue Parminter

Lord Arthur Savile's Crime
The Model Millionaire
The Sphinx without a Secret

Oscar Wilde

Text adaptation by Bill Bowler

Illustrated by David Roberts

Oscar Wilde was born in Dublin, Ireland in 1854, and studied Greek and Latin at university in Dublin and Oxford. As well as a number of short stories for adults and fairy stories for children, he wrote the novel *The Portrait of Dorian Gray* (1891). He also wrote a number of very popular comedies for the theatre, including *The Importance of Being Earnest* (1895), but is perhaps most famous for his many clever and funny sayings about life and people. He died in Paris in 1900 at the age of forty-six.

OXFORD
UNIVERSITY PRESS

BEFORE READING *LORD ARTHUR SAVILE'S CRIME*

1 **Lord Arthur's crime is murder. Who does he want to kill?**
Tick three boxes. Use a dictionary to help you.

a ☐ Lady Windermere, one of Lord Arthur's friends

b ☐ Mr Podgers, Lady Windermere's fortune teller

c ☐ Sybil Merton, the woman Lord Arthur wants to marry

Lord Arthur

d ☐ The Dean of Chichester, Lord Arthur's clever uncle

e ☐ Lord Surbiton, Lord Arthur's rich brother

f ☐ Lady Clementina, the oldest person in Lord Arthur's family

2 **Which murder methods does he use?**

a ☐ a bomb in a clock **c** ☐ drowning in a river **e** ☐ a gun
b ☐ a knife **d** ☐ poison **f** ☐ an old sword

Lord Arthur Savile's Crime

At Lady Windermere's

It was **Lady** Windermere's last party before the spring holidays. There were many more **guests** in Bentinck House – her London home – than usual. There were important men from the **government** in their best suits. All the beautiful women were wearing their most expensive dresses, and at the end of the biggest, longest room stood **Princess** Sophia of Carlsrühe, a short, heavy little lady with small black eyes and big rings on her fingers. She spoke loudly in bad French and laughed at everything that people said to her.

It was a wonderful party. There were so many different and interesting people there. Sweet ladies from old families talked with angry young men. A number of rich old artists stood on the stairs and talked together like poor art students. It was one of Lady Windermere's best nights.

Lady Windermere looked very fine with her clear white neck, her large blue eyes, like the bluest of spring flowers, and her gold hair. It was a strong gold colour, not cheap yellow, but the rich gold of sunlight.

As a young woman Lady Windermere had a number of **romantic** adventures, which made people think that she was interesting. She married three times, but because she only had one lover through all those years, the world soon stopped telling terrible stories about her. She was now forty, had no children, and enjoyed pleasing herself, which is the secret of staying young.

She was pleased when Princess Sophia stayed for hours. When the Princess left at half past eleven, Lady Windermere

lady an important woman from a good family

guest a person that you invite to your home

government the people who control a country

princess an important woman in a small country

romantic about love

began talking to her old friend the **Duchess** of Paisley.

'Where is my **palmist**?' she asked suddenly.

'Your palmist?' cried the Duchess, nearly jumping out of her seat.

'Yes, I can't live without him at the moment.'

'You are always so unusual,' said the Duchess, trying to remember what a palmist was, and hoping that it wasn't like a **manicurist**.

'He looks at my hand twice a week,' went on Lady Windermere.

'Oh dear!' said the Duchess to herself. 'He really is like a manicurist after all. How terrible to ask an uninteresting guest to a party like this! I hope he isn't English.'

'He says that I have an interesting hand,' replied Lady Windermere, 'and that it's a good thing that my **thumb** isn't any shorter, because a very short thumb means that you look on the dark side of life and prefer to leave the world behind and to be alone.'

The Duchess felt happier at once. She understood that a palmist was someone special. 'Ah, I see. And can he see the **future** in your hand too?' she asked.

'Of course,' answered Lady Windermere. 'Both the good and the bad things. I think he prefers the bad. Next year, for example, I am in great danger on the ground and at sea, so I am going to live in a large **balloon** and pull up my lunch every day in a little lunch box. It is all in my hand, you know. I think everyone should visit a palmist once a month. That way they will know what they shouldn't do. Of course they'll still do it, but it's nice to hear about bad things before they happen. Now can somebody find Mr Podgers or do I have to look for him myself?'

Lord Arthur Savile, a tall young man, stood listening to their conversation with a smile on his face. He was thinking of Sybil Merton, the woman he wanted to marry. Turning

duchess a very important woman from a very good family

palmist someone who sees the future in people's hands

manicurist someone who makes people's hands look nice

thumb the short, thick finger at the side of your hand

future what is going to happen

balloon a large ball that is full of air and flies in the sky; people ride in a basket under it

lord an important, rich man

to Lady Windermere, he said, 'I'll go and find Mr Podgers for you. But what is he like?'

'Well, he isn't unusual or romantic-looking. He's a short fat man with a large **bald** head and gold glasses. He looks like a family doctor, I'm afraid. People are very strange these days. They never look like what they are. I had a famous murderer here last year and he looked just like a nice old **vicar** and told funny stories all evening. Ah, there you are, Mr Podgers. Now, I want you to read the Duchess of Paisley's hand. Duchess, you must take off your **glove**. No, not your left hand, dear, the other one.'

'Oh, Lady Windermere. Are you sure this is all right?' said the Duchess, pulling off an old white glove.

'Of course not, nothing interesting ever is,' replied Lady Windermere, 'but that's how the world goes. Mr Podgers, this is the Duchess of Paisley. Duchess, this is Mr Podgers. And if you say that her mountain of the moon is bigger than mine I shall stop coming to you.'

bald with no hair

vicar a man who works for the church

glove a thing that you wear on your hand

'Are you sure this is all right?'

3

'I am sure there's nothing like that in my hand,' said the Duchess.

'You are right,' said Mr Podgers, looking at the little fat hand with its short, square fingers. 'You have a very small mountain of the moon. But you have a very long life **line** and will live happily for many years to come. Your head line is not really very strong, but your **heart** line—'

'Oh, tell us about her romantic adventures, Mr Podgers.'

'I'm afraid, Lady Windermere, that there isn't anything to tell. I see her feeling the same as she always has and staying with her husband.'

The Duchess looked pleased. 'Go on, Mr Podgers,' she said.

'You are very careful about spending money, I see,' he said, and Lady Windermere began to laugh loudly.

'Well, Mr Podgers, I think that you have read the Duchess's hand beautifully,' she said. 'And now you must read some other hands, too.'

So Mr Podgers read a number of other people's hands. After only a short time some guests were afraid and didn't want him even to look at their hands. But Lord Arthur Savile was interested in hearing about his future.

'Will Mr Podgers read my hand?' he asked Lady Windermere.

'Of course. But I must tell you that Sybil is coming to lunch with me tomorrow. So if Mr Podgers learns that you get angry easily or are going to be ill in later life, or have a wife in Bayswater, I shall tell her everything.'

'I'm not afraid,' answered Lord Arthur. 'Sybil knows me as well as I know her. That is why she's marrying me.'

But when Mr Podgers saw Lord Arthur's hand his face went yellow, he said nothing, his bald head shook, and his fat fingers went cold.

Lord Arthur felt afraid. 'I am waiting, Mr Podgers,' he said.

line a long thin mark; palmists look at the lines on your hand

heart the centre of feeling in somebody

'We are all waiting,' cried Lady Windermere.

Mr Podgers dropped Lord Arthur's right hand and looked carefully at his left one. His face went white. At last he looked up and pushed the corners of his mouth into a smile. 'It is the hand of a fine young man . . .' he said.

'Yes, we know that already,' said Lady Windermere. 'The question is: will he make a fine husband?'

'All fine young men do that, Lady Windermere . . . let me see . . . He will go on a journey soon . . .'

'A holiday with his new wife, of course.'

'And someone in his family will die.'

'Not his sister, I hope?' cried Lady Windermere.

'No, no,' said Mr Podgers. 'Someone not as near to him as that.'

'Oh dear! So I have nothing important to tell Sybil when she comes tomorrow.' said Lady Windermere. 'Oh well, time for supper then. Are you coming, Duchess?'

'Yes, my dear,' said the Duchess, moving slowly to the door, 'I'm tired, but I must say I have enjoyed myself, and your manicurist – palmist – was most interesting.'

Lord Arthur stood by the fire. Some guests left and some stayed. His sister walked past him to the supper table with Lord Plymdale, and Lord Arthur looked even more unhappy. He felt that something terrible was waiting in the future for him. He nearly cried to think that anything could possibly come between him and Sybil Merton.

Lord Arthur stood by the fire.

READING CHECK

Are these sentences true or false? Tick the boxes.　　**True**　**False**

a There were a lot of important people at Lady Windermere's party.　☑　☐

b Lady Windermere believes everything that Mr Podgers tells her.　☐　☐

c Lord Arthur Savile is happy when he thinks about Sybil Merton.　☐　☐

d Mr Podgers looks like a murderer.　☐　☐

e Mr Podgers reads Princess Sophia's hand at the party.　☐　☐

f Lord Arthur Savile wants Mr Podgers to read his hand.　☐　☐

g Lord Arthur Savile is going to marry a woman called Sybil.　☐　☐

h Mr Podgers tells Lord Arthur exactly what he sees in his hand.　☐　☐

WORD WORK

1 These words don't match the pictures. Correct them.

a ~~balloon~~ *palmist* **b** manicurist .... **c** palmist ....

d glove .... **e** bald .... **f** heart .... **g** thumb ....

2 Complete these sentences with words from Chapter 1.

a Lady Windermere has a house in the country and a house in London.

b Princess Sophia of Carlsrühe is a g_ _ _ _ at the party in Bentinck House.

c Lady Windermere had many r_ _ _ _ _ _ _ adventures when she was younger.

d The D_ _ _ _ _ _ of Paisley and Lady Windermere talk a lot at the party.

e Arthur Savile, a young English L_ _ _, listens to them.

f Mr Podgers can see the f_ _ _ _ _ in people's hands.

g The Duchess has a long life l_ _ _ on her hand.

h 'I haven't been to church to meet the new v_ _ _ _ yet.'

GUESS WHAT

What happens in the next chapter? Tick the boxes.

a Mr Podgers tells Lord Arthur. . . .

   1 ☐ that he is going to die soon.

   2 ☐ that he is going to kill someone.

   3 ☐ that he isn't going to marry Sybil.

b Lord Arthur decides . . .

   1 ☐ to kill himself.

   2 ☐ not to marry Sybil.

   3 ☐ to kill someone in his family.

A bloody crime

Lord Arthur Savile stood by the fire and his face was as white as stone. For the first time in his rich and careless life he felt deeply unhappy. Could Mr Podgers really see something terrible in his hand? Was it a bloody crime or something worse? Couldn't he escape from it in some way?

Suddenly Mr Podgers came back into the room When he saw Lord Arthur his face went green. For a minute both men were silent.

'The Duchess has left one of her gloves here. She asked me to bring it to her,' said Mr Podgers at last. 'Ah, I see it on that chair! Good night!'

'Mr Podgers, wait! Could you answer a question before you go? What did you see in my hand? I must know.'

'Why do you think I saw more than I told you, Lord Arthur?'

'I know that you did, and I'll pay you a hundred pounds if you tell me what it was. What is your address? I'll send you the money tomorrow.'

Mr Podgers' green eyes looked suddenly interested.

'Here is my visiting **card**,' he said, and he gave a small card to Lord Arthur, who read it:

> MR SEPTIMUS R. PODGERS
>
> PALMIST
> 103A WEST MOON STREET

card a small piece of thick paper with somebody's name and address on it

'I am there from ten until four,' said Mr Podgers.

'Be quick, now!' said Lord Arthur. 'What do you see here?' He held out his hand.

Mr Podgers closed the door.

'Very well, Lord Arthur. Please sit down.'

Ten minutes later, with a white face and wild eyes, Lord Arthur ran out of Bentinck House and down the street.

The night was very cold and windy, but his hands were hot and his face was on fire. He ran on and on. A policeman looked at him with interest when he ran past. Then a poor old man came up to ask him for some money, but when he looked into Lord Arthur's face, he felt afraid and he left the young man alone and didn't speak to him.

Suddenly Lord Arthur stopped under a street light and looked down at his hands. He thought he saw red blood on them and gave a cry.

Murder! That is what the palmist had told him. Murder! The night knew it. The wind **whispered** it in his ear. The dark corners of the street were full of it, and the houses

Lord Arthur looked down at his hands.

9

along the street laughed about it.

First he came to the **park** where he listened to the silent trees. 'Murder! Murder! I'm going to murder someone!' he said to himself, shaking terribly. He felt a strong need to stop someone in the street and tell them everything.

Then he left the park, crossed Oxford Street and walked on, down poor, narrow streets. Two women in bright cheap dresses laughed at him when he walked past them. Now and again he heard shouts and cries from the houses and he saw poor old people sitting in dark corners of the street.

At the corner of Rich Street he saw two men reading a **poster**. He crossed the street to look at it.

HAVE YOU SEEN
THIS MAN?

We are looking for a murderer. Can you help us to find a man of between thirty and forty, wearing a black coat, grey trousers and a brown hat, and with a scar near his right eye?

Police Reward £50

He read the poster many times and thought of the murderer running from the police. Perhaps one day they were going to put *his* name on a murder poster? The thought made him feel ill and he turned and hurried on.

When the sun came up he found himself in Piccadilly Circus. From there he walked slowly home to Belgrave Square, looking up at the beautiful red sky. 'I hope that there won't be a storm later in the day,' he said to himself.

By the time he got to Belgrave Square the sky was a light blue and the birds were beginning to sing in the gardens.

When Lord Arthur woke up it was twelve o'clock and the sun was high in the sky. A **servant** brought him a cup of hot chocolate in bed. He drank it and then he got ready for his morning bath. He got into the deep water quickly and lay back in it. Then he put his head right under the water

park a big garden that is open to everybody to visit

poster a big piece of paper on a wall with words on it

scar a mark on your body from an old cut

reward money that you get for helping to find someone or something

servant a person who works for someone rich

to wash away the terrible thoughts of the night before. When he got out of the bath he felt happier.

After breakfast he lay on the window seat and smoked a cigarette. On a table near him was a large photograph of Sybil Merton. She was so beautiful, with her fine small head, her soft mouth, and her dark eyes.

He couldn't marry Sybil with a future murder waiting to happen. But what could he do about it? He thought a lot, and at last he had the answer. He decided to murder someone first and then to marry Sybil. But who could he murder? Murderers, of course, usually kill their enemies, but Lord Arthur didn't really have any enemies. In the end he wrote down the names of all his friends and family on a piece of paper. After looking at this **list** for some time, he chose Lady Clementina Beauchamp, or Lady Clem, as she was called by everybody. Lady Clem was a dear old lady who lived in Curzon Street. She was one of his **cousins** on his mother's side of the family and was just the right person to murder, he decided.

Next Lord Arthur sent his servant to West Moon Street with a hundred pounds to pay Mr Podgers. After that he went out to the flower shop and bought some flowers to send to Sybil. Then he went to the **library** to read some books about different **poisons**.

He chose poison as the best way to murder Lady Clem. It was quiet and clean. After all, he didn't want his name in the newspapers. Sybil's parents weren't very modern in their way of thinking and perhaps they wouldn't like their daughter to marry a murderer if the police caught him.

In the end he found out about a poison called **aconitine**. The books explained that it worked fast, and didn't hurt you when it killed you. He wrote down how much aconitine you needed to kill someone and then he left the library and went to Saint James's Street to buy some.

list a lot of names that you write one after the other

cousin the son (or daughter) of your father's (or mother's) brother (or sister)

library a room or building where there are lots of books

poison something that kills people when they eat or drink it

aconitine /ˈækɒnɪˌtiːn/

READING CHECK

Match the first and second parts of these sentences.

a Mr Podgers . . .

b Lord Arthur asks him . . .

c Ten minutes later Lord Arthur suddenly . . .

d Mr Podgers . . .

e For hours, Lord Arthur . . .

f Very early next morning he . . .

g When he wakes up he . . .

h He decides that he . . .

i He carefully . . .

1 'What did you see in my hand?'

2 walks through the streets unhappily.

3 comes back into the room to look for something.

4 has a hot chocolate and a bath.

5 chooses someone in his family to murder.

6 runs out into the dark streets.

7 saw murder in his hand.

8 goes home to bed.

9 must murder someone before he marries Sybil.

WORD WORK

1 Find words from Chapter 2 in the cup of chocolate.

cousinservantscarcat...
poisonposterwhis
libraryparkreward
sperlist

2 Match the words from Activity 1 with the definitions.

a a small piece of thick paper .....*card*.....

b a number of words on a piece of paper ....

c a piece of paper that you put up on a wall for other people to read ....

d a room where there are lots of books ....

e a large garden in a town that everybody can visit ....

f an old cut ....

g someone who works in a rich person's house ....

h the daughter of your father's brother ....

i to speak in a quiet voice ....

j something that can kill you if you eat it ....

k money that you get for helping to find something or someone ....

GUESS WHAT

What happens in the next chapter? Tick three boxes.

a ☐ Lord Arthur kills his cousin Lady Clem.

b ☐ Lady Clem is ill but doesn't die.

c ☐ Lady Clem dies, but not from poison.

d ☐ Sybil finds out that Arthur is a murderer.

e ☐ Lord Arthur feels terrible.

f ☐ Lord Arthur marries Sybil.

g ☐ Lord Arthur doesn't marry Sybil.

3

A yellow pill

Lord Arthur walked into Pestle and Humbey's, the expensive **chemist's** shop in St James's Street, and asked Mr Pestle for some aconitine. The little man, who liked to help the lords and ladies himself when they visited his shop, said quietly that a letter from a doctor would be necessary.

But then Lord Arthur explained, 'You don't understand, Mr Pestle. It's for my large old Norwegian dog. It has to go, I'm afraid, because it's too dangerous. It **bites** my servants on the legs all the time.'

'A dangerous dog that bites servants. I see. That's all right then,' replied the chemist. 'And I must say that you know a lot about poisons, my lord,' he went on, smiling. Then he gave a yellow aconitine **pill** to Lord Arthur immediately.

Some minutes later Lord Arthur bought a beautiful little silver box in a Bond Street shop to put the yellow pill in, and then he went at once to Lady Clementina's house.

'Well, young man,' cried the old lady when he went into the room. 'Why haven't you been to see me all this time?'

'Lady Clem,' said Lord Arthur, smiling, 'I am so busy.'

'Yes. I am sure that you spend every hour of the day with Miss Sybil Merton, visiting shops and being romantic together. Why does marrying make people so romantic these days? It didn't happen when I was young.'

'Dear Lady Clem, I haven't seen Sybil for twenty-four hours. I think she is living in her favourite clothes shop.'

'Yes, and that's why you've come to see an old woman like me. I'm not stupid, you know. I have a hard life. I'm ill all the time, and the doctors only come to take my money. They don't do anything for my stomach.'

chemist a person who makes and sells medicines

bite (*past* **bit, bitten**), to cut something with your teeth

pill a small, round, hard thing that a doctor gives you to eat

'Ah,' said Lord Arthur. 'I've brought you something for that! It's a wonderful **medicine**, made in America.' And he took the silver box from his pocket and gave it to her.

'What a beautiful box, Arthur! That's so kind. And is this the medicine? It looks just like a sweet. I'll take it now.'

'Oh, no, Lady Clem,' said Lord Arthur, taking her hand. 'You mustn't do that. If you aren't feeling ill and you take this medicine you feel terrible. Wait until you're feeling bad and then take it. I'm sure it'll surprise you.'

'Very well,' said Lady Clem. 'I'd love to try it now. It looks so very good, but I'll wait until the next time that I'm ill.'

'And will that be soon?' asked Lord Arthur with interest.

'I hope not this week, but you never know.'

'So you're sure that you'll be ill this month, then?'

'Yes, I'm afraid that I will. But you're being very nice to me today, Arthur. I think that Sybil is good for you. And now I must have a rest before lunch. Goodbye, give my love to Sybil, and thank you for the medicine.'

'Don't forget to take it, Lady Clem,' said Lord Arthur, standing up.

'Of course not. And I shall tell you if I want some more.'

Lord Arthur left Lady Clem's house feeling very happy. That night he spoke to Sybil Merton. He told her that he couldn't marry her at once because he had to finish some business first. He asked her to wait until the end of the month, and he told her that everything would be fine, but that she had to wait. Early next morning he wrote a letter to her father explaining that they needed to **postpone** the **wedding** for a time. Then he left for a holiday in Venice.

His brother, Lord Surbiton, came by **yacht** from Corfu and met him there, and they spent a wonderful fortnight together. They visited Venice in the mornings, they asked people to tea on Lord Surbiton's yacht in the afternoons, and at night they ate in the best restaurants and smoked

medicine something you eat or drink to make you better when you are ill

postpone to do something at a later time

wedding the day when two people marry

yacht a small and expensive boat with sails

lots of cigarettes. But Lord Arthur wasn't happy. Every day he bought *The Times*, hoping to read about Lady Clementina's death, but every day there was nothing.

After two weeks Lord Surbiton felt bored, and both brothers went off to Ravenna. A week later Lord Arthur came back to Venice. At his hotel he found a number of **telegrams** and letters waiting for him. He read Sybil's letter first.

> Dearest Arthur,
> Terrible news! On the 17th Lady Clementina had dinner with your mother, but went home early with a bad stomach. The next day her servants found her dead in bed with a smile on her face. She has given her house in Curzon Street to you. Please come home soon.
> Lots of love,
> Sybil

Lord Arthur sent a telegram to Sybil at once to tell her that he was coming back to London. He was **sad** about Lady Clem's death, and angry with Mr Podgers for making him a murderer. But he was also deeply in love, and now he was free to marry Sybil.

When he arrived in London everything went very well. Sybil's parents were nice to him. They chose 7th June as the date of the wedding, and Sybil said to Lord Arthur, 'I hope that nothing will ever come between us again.'

Not long after, Lord Arthur and Sybil went to visit Lady Clementina's house in Curzon Street to burn old letters and papers that nobody wanted. In the middle of this Sybil gave a sudden cry of surprise.

'What have you found, Sybil?' asked Lord Arthur, smiling.

telegram a very short letter that you send very quickly

sad not happy

'This beautiful little silver box, Arthur. Can I have it?'

It was the pill box. Lord Arthur's face reddened. He remembered the poison. 'Of course you can have it,' he replied. 'I gave it to Lady Clem myself.'

'Oh, thank you, Arthur!' said Sybil, 'And can I have the sweet that's in it, too?' she went on. 'How strange! I didn't know that Lady Clem liked sweets.'

The blood left Lord Arthur's face. 'The sweet, Sybil? What do you mean?' he whispered slowly.

'There's a yellow sweet inside the box, That's all. It looks very old and I'm not really going to eat it, so don't worry. But what's the matter, Arthur? Your face is so white!'

Lord Arthur ran across the room and took the box from Sybil's hand. In it was the yellow poison pill. So he wasn't Lady Clementina's murderer after all! This news was nearly too much for him. He dropped the pill into the fire and sat down heavily on a comfortable chair with a terrible cry.

'Can I have the sweet that's in it, too?'

READING CHECK

1 What do they say?
Tick the boxes

		Mr Pestle	Lady Clem	Sybil	Lord Arthur
a	'Can I have some Aconitine?'				✔
b	'A doctor's letter is necessary.'				
c	'It's for my large old Norwegian dog.'				
d	'You know a lot about poisons.'				
e	'I'd love to try it now.'				
f	'I'm sure it'll surprise you.'				
g	'What have you found?'				
h	'Can I have the sweet that's in it?'				
i	'Your face is so white!'				

2 Put these sentences in the correct order. Number them 1–9.

a ☐ Lord Arthur puts the poison pill into a silver box.

b ☐ Lady Clem wants to take the pill at once, but Lord Arthur tells her, 'Wait until you're ill.'

c ☐ Lord Arthur gives the silver box to his aunt, Lady Clem, saying that it has some stomach medicine in it.

d ☐ Lord Arthur and Sybil go back to Lady Clem's old house in London.

e ☐ Lord Arthur buys some poison.

f ☐ Lord Arthur goes on holiday.

g ☐ Lord Arthur tells Sybil that he can't marry her for some time.

h ☐ Lord Arthur and Sybil find the poison pill in the silver box.

i ☐ Lord Arthur gets a letter from Sybil saying that Aunt Clem is dead.

18

WORD WORK

Correct the boxed words in these sentences. They all come from Chapter 3.

a She took a bill because she felt ill. ..pill........

b I felt very sat when my cousin died. ....

c I want to have a white bedding in a church. ....

d Careful that dog doesn't site you. It's got very big teeth. ....

e Mr Pestle works as a chemical. ....

f They had to postman the party for a week. ....

g You must take some of this medical before you go to bed. ....

h Lord Surbiton goes to Venice by yak. ....

i They sent me a telephone to tell me about my cousin dying. ....

GUESS WHAT

What happens in the next chapter? Tick the pictures.

a Lord Arthur tries to kill . . .

1 himself. **2** Lady Windermere. **3** his uncle. **4** Mr Podgers.

b Lord Arthur is going to use . . .

1 poison. **2** a knife. **3** a bomb. **4** a gun.

4

A bomb in a clock

Mr Merton was not very happy when Lord Arthur Savile postponed his daughter's wedding for a second time. Mrs Merton was very angry and spoke to her daughter about not marrying Lord Arthur, but Sybil's heart was full of love, and she agreed to wait for the wedding.

Lord Arthur was **disappointed** about the poison not working, but he decided to try again. This time he felt that a **bomb** was the best thing to use. He got out his list of family and friends and after thinking very carefully, he decided to murder his **uncle**, the **Dean** of Chichester.

The Dean was a very clever man who loved clocks. He had a house full of them. Some were four hundred years old, and some were very modern.

Lord Arthur decided that the easiest way to kill his uncle was by putting a bomb in a clock and sending it to him. But where can you buy a bomb?

Then he remembered his friend **Count** Rouvaloff, a young Russian who sometimes went to Lady Windermere's parties. Rouvaloff was writing a book about Peter the Great, but people said that he was a **revolutionary**. Lord Arthur drove to the Russian's rooms in Bloomsbury to ask him for his help.

'I want a bomb!' he said. 'Where can I get one?'

'Lord Arthur,' replied Rouvaloff, 'I never knew that you were so interested in **politics**.'

'My dear Rouvaloff, politics don't interest me,' answered Lord Arthur. 'It is family business only.'

Count Rouvaloff looked at him in surprise. Then, seeing that the young English lord truly meant what he said, he

disappointed unhappy because you don't get what you want

bomb a thing which explodes noisily and can kill people

uncle your father's (or mother's) brother

dean an important man of the church

count an important man

revolutionary someone who fights against a government, often with guns and bombs

politics the way people choose a government

wrote an address on a piece of paper, put his name at the bottom, and gave it to him.

'The English police would love to have this address, my friend,' he said.

'Well, they won't get it from me,' replied Lord Arthur, laughing, and he shook hands with Rouvaloff and ran downstairs.

Looking at the paper in his hand, he went at once to Soho. There, near Greek Street, he found a place called Bayle's Court. He knocked on the door of a little green house and a strange **foreign** man asked him what he wanted. Lord Arthur gave him Count Rouvaloff's paper. The man took Lord Arthur into a dirty front room.

After a few minutes Mr Winckelkopf, as he was called in England, came into the room with a fork in one hand.

'Count Rouvaloff told me to come,' said Lord Arthur. 'My name is Mr Robert Smith, and I want to buy a clock with a bomb in it.'

'Pleased to meet you, Lord Arthur,' said the little German, laughing. 'Don't be surprised. It's my job to know everybody, and I remember seeing you one evening at Lady Windermere's. I hope she is well. Would you like to sit with me? I am just finishing my breakfast.'

Lord Arthur was very surprised that Mr Winckelkopf knew his name, but he followed him into the back room of the house, and sat and talked in the friendliest way with this famous revolutionary.

'Clocks with bombs in are not good for foreign murders,' said the little German. 'Trains are often late and clock-bombs can easily **explode** before they get to where they are going. But if you want a bomb in a clock for use in England I can get you one with no trouble. Can I ask you who you want to kill with it? If it's a policeman or a Scotland Yard detective then I'm afraid I can't help you.

foreign not from your country

explode to break suddenly with a very loud noise

21

monster a large, horrible animal

The English detectives are our best friends. Because they are so stupid, we can do everything we want here. We don't want to kill any of them.'

'No, no,' said Lord Arthur, 'I don't want to kill a policeman. The clock is for the Dean of Chichester.'

'Do you feel strongly about the Church, Lord Arthur?'

'No, no, he is my uncle. This is family business, not Church business.'

'How does it explode?'

'I see,' said Winckelkopf and he left the room and came back a few minutes later with a beautiful French clock. On top of it there was a little revolutionary woman standing on a terrible **monster** with six heads. 'Here is your bomb.'

'That's just what I want! But how does it explode?'

'That is my little secret,' said the German. 'Just tell me two things. What time do you want it to arrive at the Dean's house? And what time do you want it to explode? I will do the rest.'

22

'Can you send it off at once?' asked Lord Arthur.

'Not today. I have some important work for some friends in Moscow.'

'Well, could you send it either tomorrow night or Thursday morning? And I'd like it to explode at twelve o'clock on Friday, please,' said Lord Arthur. 'The Dean always has lunch at that time. Now, how much is that?'

'Well, the clock was four pounds, and the bomb inside will be a pound. For myself, nothing. Lord Arthur, I am only too happy to help one of Count Rouvaloff's friends. And I do not work for money.'

Lord Arthur put five pounds on the table, thanked the little German for his time, left the house and went back home feeling very happy.

For the next two days Lord Arthur was terribly excited. On Friday at twelve o'clock he went to his **club** to wait for the news. All afternoon Lord Arthur waited, but no news came. At four o'clock the evening newspapers arrived and Lord Arthur read them all from front to back, but there was nothing about someone murdering the Dean of Chichester with an exploding clock. There was no news from Chichester at all. He felt very disappointed.

The next day he went back to Bayle's Court in Soho to see Mr Winckelkopf again. The little German was very sorry about the accident and he **promised** to send another clock-bomb to the Dean of Chichester as soon as possible. 'And I don't want any more money, Lord Arthur,' he said. But by now Lord Arthur didn't really **trust** bombs to do the job well, and even Winckelkopf agreed that it was difficult to find good **gunpowder**.

'I'm sure that something went wrong with the clock, Lord Arthur,' he said. 'But perhaps the gunpowder will explode without it. I haven't lost hope.'

But Lord Arthur was not very hopeful.

club a place where gentlemen meet

promise to say that you will certainly do something

trust to feel sure that something will happen as you think it will

gunpowder powder that explodes

READING CHECK

Correct nine more mistakes in the chapter summary.

Mr Merton ~~is~~ *isn't* very happy when Lord Arthur postpones his wedding to Sybil again. Lord Arthur decides to kill his grandfather, the Dean of Chichester. The Dean hates clocks and Lord Arthur decides to use a bomb in a book to kill him. He visits a French revolutionary Count Rouvaloff in Bloomsbury for help. He gives Lord Arthur an address in Chichester. Lord Arthur goes there and meets Mr Winckelkopf, a German revolutionary. Winckelkopf doesn't want to kill any English postmen. But Lord Arthur tells him that the murder which he is planning is family business. Then Winckelkopf sells Lord Arthur a beautiful German clock with a revolutionary man standing on it and a bomb inside it. Lord Arthur wants the bomb to explode when the Dean is having breakfast on Friday. In Friday's newspapers there is no news from Chichester of the murder of the Dean.

bomb club Count
Dean ~~disappointed~~
explode foreign gunpowder
politics monster promises
uncle trust revolutionaries

WORD WORK

Use the words in the clock to complete the sentences on page 25.

a When Lord Arthur finds that he didn't murder Lady Clem, he feels very disappointed.

b He decides to buy a _ _ _ _ that will _ _ _ _ _ _ _ and kill his _ _ _ _ _ _, the _ _ _ _ of Chichester.

c He visits _ _ _ _ _ Rouvaloff and Winckelkopf, two _ _ _ _ _ _ _ _ men who are _ _ _ _ _ _ _ _ _ _ _ _ _ _ _ .

d Lord Arthur isn't interested in _ _ _ _ _ _ _ _ _ .

e He buys a clock with a bomb in it and a _ _ _ _ _ _ _ with six heads on the top.

f On Friday Lord Arthur waits at his _ _ _ _ in London to read the news from Chichester in the newspaper, but there is nothing.

g Winckelkopf _ _ _ _ _ _ _ _ _ to send a second clock with more _ _ _ _ _ _ _ _ _ _ in it, but Lord Arthur doesn't _ _ _ _ _ bombs any more.

GUESS WHAT

What does Lord Arthur do next? Tick three pictures.

a ☐ He tells Sybil that he can't marry her.

c ☐ He decides to buy a different kind of bomb from Mr Winckelkopf.

b ☐ He reads a letter from his cousin about the clock.

d ☐ He has dinner with his brother at his club.

e ☐ He meets Mr Podgers again.

5

By the River Thames

Two days after his second visit to Mr Winckelkopf, Lord Arthur's mother, the Duchess, showed him a letter.

'You must read this,' she said.

Lord Arthur took the letter and read it.

The Dean's House, Chichester
17th May

My Dearest Aunt,

Thank you for your last letter. We have had a fine time this week with a clock which someone sent to father last Thursday. It came in a box from London, and father is sure that the person who sent it knows his work, because not very long ago he spoke about Liberty in church and he later wrote it all down in a book called 'Is Liberty too free?' and this clock had a woman dressed as Liberty on the top. I didn't think she looked very nice, but father said that the clock was a French Revolutionary piece and that, for her time, little Miss Liberty was all right. Well, our servant Parker took the clock out of its box, and father put it in the library. Then, on Friday at twelve o'clock, we were all sitting in the library when the clock whirred and exploded, some smoke came out from under Miss Liberty and she fell off and broke her nose on the floor. Maria cried, but it was very funny and James and I laughed, and father laughed too. When we looked inside the clock we saw that it was an alarm clock. You can turn it to any time, put some gunpowder in, and it

aunt your father's (or mother's) sister

liberty being free to go where you want and to do what you want

whirr to make a noise like the moving parts of a machine

alarm clock a clock that makes a noise to wake you up

26

explodes when you want. Father said that it couldn't stay in the library because it was too noisy, so James took it into the schoolroom and he now does nothing but make it whirr and explode all day long. Do you think that Arthur would like one of these clocks for his wedding present? Perhaps they are in all the shops in London these days. Father is sure that they will sell well, for they show that Liberty can't be on top for ever and must fall down.

Reggie has just made the clock explode again, and father says that the boys must take it outside. I don't think he likes it very much now. But he is happy that people read his books, and the clock is very cleverly made.

Father sends his love, and James, Reggie and Maria send their love too.

Lots of love, dear aunt, from your **niece**,
Jane Percy

Lord Arthur looked sad after reading the letter and his mother laughed. 'My dear Arthur,' she said, 'I shall never show you a young lady's letter again! But what do you think of these alarm clocks? They sound wonderful.'

'I don't think they're so wonderful,' said Lord Arthur, with a sad smile, and he left the room. Upstairs he lay down on his bed, his eyes full of **tears**.

'I've tried twice, but I still haven't murdered anybody. I must tell Sybil that I can't marry her,' he thought.

He knew that it would hurt her, but with time she would forget him. For himself all he wanted was to die.

At half past seven he dressed and went to his club. His brother was there with a group of other young men and he had to have dinner with them. He listened to their stories

niece your sister's (or brother's) daughter

tear the water that comes from your eye when you cry

umbrella a thing that you hold over your head to keep you dry when it rains

It was Mr Podgers the palmist!

and conversation without interest, and after coffee he left the club. When he walked past the front desk on his way out they gave him a letter. It was from Mr Winckelkopf and it asked him to come to Bayle's Court the next day. He promised to show him an **umbrella** bomb that exploded when you opened it – the latest thing from Geneva. Lord Arthur threw the letter away. He really didn't trust bombs now, and he didn't want to murder anybody.

He walked down to the River Thames and sat by a bridge looking out at the dark waters of the Thames below him for hours. The clock at Westminster sounded midnight and still Lord Arthur watched the river.

At two o'clock he got up and began to walk east. Everything looked strange in the moonlight, a picture of black and silver. Then suddenly he saw a man in front of him looking over the wall down into the river. The man looked up and Lord Arthur saw his face under the streetlight. It was Mr Podgers the palmist!

A clever idea came to Lord Arthur. He walked silently up behind Mr Podgers, took him by the legs, and pushed him over the wall and down into the Thames. There was a cry, the noise of something falling into the river, and then nothing but the palmist's tall hat moving round and round on the water. Then that too went down.

'Lost something?' came a voice. It was a policeman.

'No,' said Lord Arthur. 'Nothing important.'

Two days later he read the news in the evening newspaper.

FAMOUS PALMIST DIES IN THAMES

Yesterday morning at seven o'clock a guest from the Ship Hotel found the body of Septimus Podgers (the famous palmist) by the River Thames. The palmist's friends feel sure that he killed himself because he was working too hard.

Lord Arthur ran out of his club with the paper in his hand and went to Sybil's house. 'My dearest, let's have our wedding tomorrow!' he cried.

'But, Arthur, my dress isn't ready yet!' she laughed.

Three weeks later the Dean of Chichester married them in St Peter's church, and the best people came to the wedding.

Years later, when they had two children, Lady Windermere went to visit them at their country home and she talked to Lady Sybil out in the garden.

'Do you remember Mr Podgers?' she said. 'I was very disappointed when he died. Didn't he see that coming to him? I don't think much of palmists these days.'

'Oh, Lady Windermere, don't say anything against palmists in front of Arthur,' said Lady Sybil.

'Why not?'

'Because,' said Lord Arthur, coming round the corner of the house, 'a palmist brought us together.' And he looked lovingly into his wife's dark eyes.

READING CHECK

1 Match the sentences with the people.

1 Jane Percy

3 Lord Arthur

5 Sybil

7 Mr Podgers

a . . . laughs when the clock bomb explodes in his library.

b . . . writes funnily about the clock bomb arriving in Chichester.

c . . . goes to his club for dinner feeling very sad.

d . . . and a group of other young men are there.

e . . . sends a letter to Lord Arthur.

f . . . is in the street near the River Thames.

g . . . pushes him into the river, where he dies.

h . . . asks Sybil to marry him.

i . . . marries Lord Arthur and Sybil in Saint Peter's church.

j . . . goes to visit Arthur and Sybil later.

k . . . tells Lady Windermere that Arthur believes in palmists.

2 The Dean of Chichester

4 Mr Winckelkopf

6 Lady Windermere

8 Lord Arthur's brother

2 Complete the police report.

METROPOLITAN POLICE • REPORT FORM

a **Name of the dead person:** Septimus Podgers

b **What was his job?**

c **Where did he live?**

d **What did he look like?**

e **Where was the body found?**

f **What time was the body found?**

g **Who found it?**

h **How did the person die?**

WORD WORK

Use words from Chapter 5 to complete the sentences.
Make changes where necessary.

a Jane Percy writes a letter to explain about the clock whirring and then exploding, and about Miss _ _ _ _ _ _ _ falling off.

b Jane Percy is Lord Arthur's cousin and a _ _ _ _ _ of the Duchess.

c She thinks that Mr Winckelkopf's bomb clock is an _ _ _ _ _ _ _ _ _ _ .

d Lord Arthur's mother is Jane Percy's _ _ _ _ _ .

e Lord Arthur's eyes are full of _ _ _ _ _ when he thinks that he can't marry Sybil.

f Mr Winckelkopf writes a letter to Lord Arthur about some new _ _ _ _ _ _ _ _ _ bombs that have arrived from Geneva.

GUESS WHAT

What happens after the story ends? Tick the boxes.

a ☐ Mr Podgers comes back from the dead to visit Lord Arthur.

b ☐ Lady Windermere decides people who can tell you what you are thinking are boring, too.

c ☐ One of Lord Arthur's children wants to be a palmist.

d ☐ Lord Arthur tells Sybil the true story about Mr Podgers.

e ☐ Mr Winckelkopf dies in a bomb attack.

f ☐ Sybil meets a palmist who tells her to murder her husband.

g ☐ The Duchess of Paisley's husband dies and she marries again.

h ☐ Lord Surbiton marries Jane Percy.

i ☐ The Dean of Chichester finds out that Lord Arthur tried to kill him.

BEFORE READING *THE MODEL MILLIONAIRE*

1 Match the words with the pictures. Use a dictionary to help you.

beggar millionaire happy sad poor rich young
old generous mean charming hard-hearted

THE OLD BEGGAR

HUGHIE ERSKINE

a

....

....

....

....

....

b

....

....

....

....

2 What happens between these two men in the story? Tick two boxes.

a ☐ Hughie Erskine gives money to the old beggar.

b ☐ The old beggar steals money from Hughie Erskine.

c ☐ Hughie Erskine becomes rich after the old beggar helps him.

d ☐ Something different. What?

The Model Millionaire

1

A poor young man

Hughie Erskine was a **charming** young man with no money. Now, if you aren't rich, being charming doesn't help you much. Hughie, sadly, did not understand this. Poor Hughie! With his brown hair and his grey eyes, he was a great favourite with women, and men liked him too. But he wasn't very clever and he wasn't good at making money. When his father died, all that Hughie got from him was an old army **sword** and some old books. He put the sword on his wall, and the books into his small library. Luckily one of his aunts gave him two hundred pounds a year to live on. He tried to get a job, but nothing agreed with him. He worked in a bank for six months, but money had no interest for him. Then he tried selling tea, but it was too foreign for him. After that he went into selling **wine**, but he didn't really have a taste for it. In the end he did nothing.

To make things worse, Hughie was also in love. The girl that he loved was Laura Merton, the daughter of an old army man, once a **colonel** out in India. Since coming back to England the Colonel had terrible stomach trouble and was angry all the time. Laura loved Hughie and Hughie loved Laura, but they didn't have sixpence between them. The Colonel liked Hughie, but he didn't want Laura to marry a poor young man.

'We'll talk about the wedding when you've got ten thousand pounds in the bank,' he often said. Hughie became very sad after conversations like that and had to talk to Laura for hours before he felt happy again.

charming nice to other people

sword a long, sharp knife for fighting

wine a red or white alcoholic drink made from grapes

colonel an important soldier in the army

paint to put
different colours
on paper to make a
picture

beggar a person
who asks other
people for money
in the street

model a person
who sits or stands
so that an artist
can paint him

*'What a
wonderful
model!'*

One morning, on his way to Holland Park, where Laura and her father lived, Hughie went to see his great friend Alan Trevor. Trevor was a strange-looking, untidy man with wild red hair, but he **painted** wonderful pictures, and everybody in town wanted to buy them.

When Hughie came in, he found Trevor busy finishing a picture of a **beggar**. The picture was as big as the beggar himself, for the old man was sitting in one corner of the room. He had a long, sad face and was wearing a thin old brown coat which had a number of holes in it. On his feet he wore cheap old shoes and in his hand he held out a soft old hat, waiting for people to put money in it.

'What a wonderful **model**!' cried Hughie.

'Yes, he is wonderful, isn't he?' agreed Trevor. 'You don't find beggars like him every day. He's got a face out of a picture by a famous Spanish or Dutch painter – Velasquez or Rembrandt perhaps.'

'Poor old beggar!' said Hughie. 'What a sad face he's got! But I'm sure that it will help you to sell your picture for a lot of money.'

'Of course,' said Trevor. 'Nobody wants to buy a picture of a happy beggar!'

'How much does a painter's model get for his work?' asked Hughie, sitting down in a comfortable chair.

'Twelve pence an hour.'

'And how much will you get for the painting?'

'Two thousand pounds.'

'Well I think that your model needs to get a **percentage** of what you get. It isn't easy sitting there and not moving for hours, you know.'

'But I have to stand here for hours looking and painting, and buying the paint itself is a job too you know. But just be quiet now. I'm busy.'

After some time a servant came in and told Trevor that the man who made his **frames** was outside and wanted to speak to him.

'Don't go away, Hughie,' said Trevor on his way out of the room. 'I'll be back in a minute or two.'

With Trevor out of the room for a time, the old beggar got up and moved his arms and legs. Hughie felt very sorry for him and he put his hands in his pockets to see what money he had on him. All he could find was a pound and a few pence.

'Poor old man,' he thought kindly. 'He needs this money more than I need it.' And he went over and put the pound into the old man's hand.

The old man looked at him and smiled strangely. 'Thank you, young man. Thank you,' he said.

Almost at once Trevor came back, and Hughie left to go to Laura's house. His face reddened when he thought of his present to the old beggar.

'Oh, Hughie, you are stupid,' cried Laura later when Hughie told her all about it, 'Why did you give a pound away?'

percentage a hundredth part of something (%)

frame the piece of wood around the outside of a door or a picture

READING CHECK

Are these sentences true or false? Tick the boxes.

		True	False
a	Hughie Erskine has got lots of money.	☐	✔
b	He is a great favourite with women.	☐	☐
c	He is in love with Laura Merton.	☐	☐
d	Laura's father hates Hughie.	☐	☐
e	One day Hughie visits his painter friend Alan Trevor.	☐	☐
f	Alan is painting a picture of a young beggar.	☐	☐
g	The model for the painting is sitting in the room.	☐	☐
h	When Alan leaves the room, Hughie gives the man ten pounds.	☐	☐
i	Laura is angry with Hughie for giving money to a beggar.	☐	☐

WORD WORK

Find words in the artist's paints to complete the sentences.

a Hughie Erskine is a c*harming* young man.

b Hughie's father left him an old
s _ _ _ _ when he died.

c Laura's father was a
c _ _ _ _ _ _
in India.

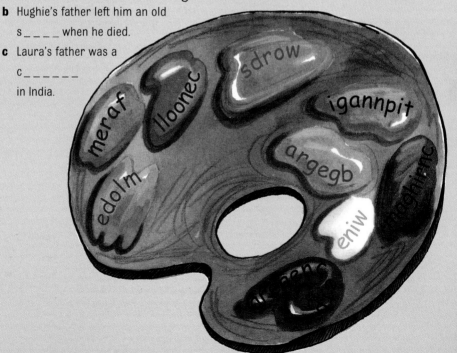

d Hughie tries selling w _ _ _ , but he isn't very good at it.

e When Hughie visits him, Alan Trevor is p _ _ _ _ _ _ _ a picture.

f The picture is of a sad old b _ _ _ _ _ _ .

g The m _ _ _ _ is in the studio too; he's an old man.

h Hughie feels that the old man should get a p _ _ _ _ _ _ _ _ _ of the money that Alan gets for his painting.

i When Alan's painting of the old man is finished he is going to put a nice f _ _ _ _ round it.

GUESS WHAT

What happens in the next chapter?

Tick the boxes.	Yes	No
a Hughie becomes rich.	☐	☐
b Hughie learns that the beggar is rich.	☐	☐
c Alan Trevor paints a picture of Hughie.	☐	☐
d Hughie gets married to Laura.	☐	☐
e Laura leaves Hughie.	☐	☐

2
An interesting model

That evening, Hughie walked to his club at about 11 o'clock. He found his friend Alan Trevor in the smoking room there, with a drink in his hand.

'Did you finish that picture of the beggar?' Hughie asked.

'Oh yes, I finished it and now it's in its frame and ready to sell. Oh, and the old model himself was very interested in you. I had to tell him all about you. He wanted to know who you were, where you lived, and how much money you got a year.'

'My dear Alan,' cried Hughie. 'I don't want to find the old man outside my door when I go home. But you're just **joking**, of course. Poor old thing! I'd like to do something for him. I think it's terrible for anybody to be so sad. I've got lots of old clothes at home. Do you think he'd like some of them? His coat was full of holes.'

'Yes, but he looks wonderful in it. I really wouldn't like to paint him in an expensive new coat. But I'll tell him what you've said.'

'You painters have no **feelings**!' said Hughie.

'A painter's heart is in his head,' replied Trevor. 'And now tell me about Laura. How is she? My old model was very interested in her.'

'You didn't tell him about her too, did you?'

'Of course I did. He knows all about the Colonel with the bad stomach and the hard heart, and all about your beautiful Laura and the £10,000, too!'

'So you told that old beggar everything about me, did you?' cried Hughie angrily, and his face went very red.

'My dear boy,' said Trevor, smiling, 'that old beggar, as

joke to say things that are not serious, or are funny

feeling something that you feel inside yourself

you call him, is one of the richest men in Europe. With the money that he's got in the bank he could buy all of London without thinking twice. He has houses in London, Paris, Berlin, Vienna, Moscow, Rome, Madrid and New York, and he always uses gold plates on his dinner table.'

'What do you mean?' cried Hughie.

'What I say,' said Trevor. 'The old man that you saw today in my house was **Baron** Hausberg. He's one of my greatest friends. He buys lots of my pictures, and a month ago he asked me to paint him as a beggar. I really don't know why. He's a **millionaire**, and when someone's a millionaire you don't ask questions. But I must say that I thought he looked wonderful in his beggar's coat. Or my beggar's coat if you want to know. He was wearing some old clothes that I bought years ago in Spain.'

'Baron Hausberg!' cried Hughie. 'Oh, no! Because I felt so sorry for him, I gave him a pound!' and he sat back in

baron an important man from a very rich old family

millionaire someone who has more than a million pounds

That old beggar is one of the richest men in Europe.

his chair with a very long face.

'You gave him a pound!' laughed Trevor. 'Well, you won't see that again. The Baron's business is other people's money, you know.'

'Why didn't you tell me he was a millionaire?' said Hughie angrily.

'Well, to start with, Hughie,' said Trevor, 'I didn't know that you like giving money to strangers. I can understand a man who wants to **kiss** a beautiful young lady model. But giving a pound to a smelly old beggar – that's too much! And also when you arrived at my place, I wasn't sure what to do. The Baron likes his little secrets. So I thought it was better not to tell you his name. I mean, he wasn't in his best clothes!'

'I'm sure he thinks that I'm really stupid!' said Hughie.

'No, you're wrong there. He was very happy when he left my house. He couldn't stop smiling to himself. I didn't understand at first why he wanted to find out everything about you, but I can see why he was interested in you now. He'll put your money in the bank for you, Hughie, and every six months he'll pay you a small percentage, and that way he'll have a wonderful story to tell his friends after dinner.'

'Oh dear!' said Hughie. 'I feel ill. I'm going home to bed. Alan, please don't tell anyone about this. If all my friends find out, I shall never come to the club again.'

'Hughie, wait a minute. Don't run away now. I think that giving a pound to someone that you thought was a beggar was a very **generous** thing to do,' laughed Trevor, but Hughie left the club and walked home, feeling very unhappy.

kiss to touch lovingly with your mouth

generous always ready to give things to other people

The next morning, when Hughie was eating his breakfast, there was a knock at the door and his servant brought in a card. He read it with interest.

MR GUSTAVE NAUDIN

(Baron Hausberg's friend)

'Oh dear. I'm sure that he wants me to say sorry for what I did to the Baron yesterday,' thought Hughie.

He told his servant to show Mr Naudin in. A nice old **gentleman** with glasses and grey hair came into the room.

'Are you Mr Erskine?' he asked in a soft, kind voice.

'I am,' replied Hughie.

'I have come from Baron Hausberg,' the old gentleman went on. 'The Baron—'

'Look, please tell the Baron that I'm terribly sorry for what happened yesterday,' said Hughie, and his face was suddenly very red.

'The Baron,' said the gentleman with a smile, 'has asked me to bring you this.' And he took an **envelope** from his pocket and gave it to Hughie.

On the outside of the envelope Hughie read, 'A wedding present to Hugh Erskine and Laura Merton, from an old beggar.' Inside the envelope was a **cheque** for £10,000.

When Hughie married Laura, Alan Trevor was the **best man** and stood at his friend's side in church. And Baron Hausberg said a few words at the wedding breakfast, too.

Trevor turned to Hughie with a smile when the Baron sat down. 'What a lucky young man you are!' he said. 'You don't find millionaire models every day, but a **model** millionaire is even harder to find.'

gentleman a man from a rich family who does not need to work

envelope a paper cover that you put a letter in

cheque a piece of paper from a bank that promises to pay money to someone

best man a man at a wedding who helps the man who is getting married

model very good

ACTIVITIES

READING CHECK

Choose the words to complete the sentences correctly.

a Hughie goes to his | club / mother's house / old school | and finds Alan Trevor there.

b Hughie wants to give the old man some of his | old books. / clothes. / shoes. |

c Alan says the old man was very interested in | Laura. / tea. / wine. |

d Alan told the old man all about the | artist / colonel / doctor | with the hard heart, and about the | house / job / money | that Hughie needs before he can marry Laura.

e In the end Alan tells Hughie that his model was a | banker. / beggar. / millionaire. |

f Hughie is afraid that his friends will think that he is | generous. / ill. / stupid. |

g The next morning a friend of Baron Hausberg visits Hughie and gives him some money as a | birthday / Christmas / wedding | present from the Baron.

42

WORD WORK

Use words from Chapter 2 of *The Model Millionaire* to complete Hughie Erskine's diary. Make changes where necessary.

I had a (a) f e e l i n g that there was something wrong when I told Alan Trevor about giving that old beggar in his studio my old clothes. He laughed and said 'Hughie, you're (b) j _ _ _ _ _!' Then he said 'That wasn't really an old beggar, it was (c) B _ _ _ _ Hausberg, and he's a (d) m _ _ _ _ _ _ _ _ _ _. When I told Alan about the pound I gave to Hausberg, he laughed louder. 'Oh, very (e) g _ _ _ _ _ _ _ of you, Hughie!'

Well, I was worried about the Baron. Did he think I was stupid or rude giving him a pound like that? But the next day a nice (f) g _ _ _ _ _ _ _ _ called Gustave Naudin came to my house with an (g) e _ _ _ _ _ _ _ from the Baron. Inside was a (h) c _ _ _ _ _ for ten thousand pounds!

The Baron is a (i) m _ _ _ _ millionaire – he is rich and kind. Because of his money I could marry Laura. Alan was (j) b _ _ _ _ _ _ at my wedding. And Laura (k) k _ _ _ _ _ _ the old Baron, who also came to the wedding, to say thank you to him.

GUESS WHAT

What happens after the story ends? Tick the boxes.

a ☐ Hughie gets a good job after he marries Laura, and he becomes rich.

b ☐ Hughie never gets a job but he and Laura are happy.

c ☐ The Colonel dies and leaves all his money to poor people in India.

d ☐ The Baron dies and leaves all his paintings to Hughie.

e ☐ Alan Trevor becomes famous and rich.

f ☐ Hughie becomes a millionaire but gives all his money to beggars.

g ☐ Laura starts to like expensive clothes and spends all their money.

h ☐ Alan Trevor starts to paint wedding pictures and becomes a millionaire.

BEFORE READING *THE SPHINX WITHOUT A SECRET*

1 **Tick the words below that best describe the woman in the picture. Use a dictionary to help you.**

☐ boring

☐ mysterious

☐ romantic

☐ heartless

☐ charming

☐ lonely

☐ angry

☐ sad

☐ happy

2 **This is Lord Murchison. Why is he interested in the woman in the picture?**

a ☐ His brother is going to marry her.

b ☐ She's a famous singer.

c ☐ She's going to marry him.

d ☐ He falls in love with her when he first sees her.

The Sphinx without a Secret

1

The woman in the yellow carriage

One afternoon I was sitting outside a **café** in a Paris street watching the world go by. Over my drink I watched young and old, millionaires and beggars, walking past me and I thought about how different people's lives are. Then, suddenly, I heard someone calling my name. I turned round and saw Lord Murchison. He was a very great friend from my **university** days.

'Murchison!' I cried. 'I haven't seen you since we were at Oxford together and that's nearly ten years ago. I'm so happy to meet you again!'

We shook hands warmly. I remembered him well. I liked him a lot at Oxford. He was **handsome**, he loved going to parties, and above all he had a good heart. My other university friends and I always said that he was a model gentleman but for one thing – he always told the **truth**. But secretly I think that we **admired** him for being so truthful.

But he was different now to how I remembered him. There were lines on his face, and I could see that he was worried about something. I knew him well and felt sure that he wasn't losing sleep about modern politics, or about changes in the church. I decided then that a woman had come into his life.

'You've changed a lot, Murchison,' I said. 'Are you married?'

'No,' he answered. 'You have to understand a woman if you want to marry her, and I'm afraid I don't understand women at all.'

'Women want men to love them, not to understand them.'

café a place where people go to drink coffee

university people study here after they finish school

handsome good-looking

truth what is true

admire to think that somebody is very good

45

'Well, I can't love a woman if I don't trust her.'

'You have a mystery in your life,' I said. 'Tell me about it.'

'Let's drive somewhere,' he answered. 'I can't talk freely here with all these people round us.'

We got up to look for a **carriage**.

'No, not a yellow carriage. Let's take that dark green one.'

'Where shall we go?' I asked, getting into the green carriage.

'It doesn't matter!' he answered. 'Let's go to a restaurant far from the centre of town. We can eat there and you can tell me about yourself.'

'I want to hear about you first,' I said. 'Tell me your mystery.'

He took out a photograph of a woman and put it in my hand.

'What do you think of her?' he asked.

I looked at the photograph carefully. She was a romantic woman with large eyes and long hair. I felt that her face held a secret, but was it a good secret or a terrible one? Her smile wasn't sweet, but full of mystery.

'She looks very interesting,' I said. 'Tell me about her.'

'After dinner,' he said, and began to talk of other things.

When our coffee and cigarettes arrived at the dinner table I again asked Murchison to tell me about the woman in the photograph. He sat back in his chair and told me his story.

⟩⟨⟩⟨⟩

One afternoon I was walking down Bond Street in London at about five o'clock. There were lots of carriages on the road and the traffic was moving very slowly. I saw a little yellow carriage near me and when I walked by it, the face from the photograph that I showed you earlier looked out at me. I was immediately interested. I couldn't stop thinking of that face all night. And the next day I walked up and

carriage an old kind of car that horses pull

down Bond Street but I couldn't find the lady again. I began to think that she was only a **dream** in my head.

A week later I went to Lady de Rastail's house. On the **invitation** it said 'Dinner at eight o'clock', but at half past eight we were still waiting. At last a servant came in and said, 'Lady Alroy has arrived!'

'The face looked out at me.'

Then Lady Alroy walked slowly into the room, and I saw at once that she was the mystery woman. She wore a beautiful silvery grey dress and the stones in the rings on her fingers were like lovely moons.

I felt happy when she sat next to me at dinner and just for something to say, I said, 'I think I saw you in Bond Street a week ago, Lady Alroy.'

Her face went white and she replied in a quiet voice, 'Please don't speak so loudly; someone will hear you!'

I was disappointed that our first conversation was going so badly and began to talk of the theatre. She spoke in a quiet, musical voice, but didn't say much. I felt that she was afraid of people listening. I fell deeply, stupidly in love, and the mystery about her made her twice as interesting.

After dinner, I asked her when I could visit her.

'Tomorrow at a quarter to five,' she whispered, and then she left.

Later I learnt from Lady de Rastail that she was a **widow** with a beautiful house in Park Lane, but that was all I could find out about her.

dream a picture that you see in your head when you are sleeping

invitation a letter asking you to go somewhere

widow a woman whose husband is dead

READING CHECK

1 Are these sentences about Lord Murchison true or false? Tick the boxes.

		True	False
a	He was handsome as a young man.	✔	☐
b	He hated going to parties in his university days.	☐	☐
c	He had a good heart.	☐	☐
d	He was never truthful.	☐	☐
e	Now he looks tired.	☐	☐
f	He is married.	☐	☐
g	He is very interested in Lady Alroy.	☐	☐

2 Correct the mistakes in these sentences.

a The storyteller is sitting outside a café in a ~~London~~ *Paris* street when the story starts.

b The storyteller and Lord Murchison were friends at Cambridge University.

c They go to a restaurant near the centre of town to talk.

d Lord Murchison shows the storyteller a photograph of a woman with short hair.

e Before dinner Lord Murchison talks about Lady Alroy – the woman in the photograph.

f He saw her first in Bond Street, sitting in a little green carriage.

g He met her again at Lady de Rastail's house when they went there for breakfast.

h She was happy when he said, 'I saw you in Bond Street.'

i She didn't want to meet him again the next day.

WORD WORK

Match words in Chapter 1 of *The Sphinx without a Secret* with these definitions.

a A woman whose husband has died and who has not married again. ...widow......

b A letter asking you to go somewhere or do something. ....

c A story which happens in your mind when you are asleep. ....

d A vehicle with wheels that is pulled by horses. ....

e To like somebody or something very much. ....

f What is true. ....

g Good-looking, attractive. ....

h A high level of education for students who have finished school. ....

i A small restaurant that serves drinks and light meals. ....

GUESS WHAT

What do you think happens in the next chapter? Tick two boxes.

a ☐ Lord Murchison understands Lady Alroy's mystery.

b ☐ Lord Murchison doesn't trust Lady Alroy.

c ☐ Lady Alroy tells the truth.

d ☐ Lord Murchison asks Lady Alroy to marry him.

e ☐ Lady Alroy dies of a broken heart.

2

The house in Cumnor Street

I drank another cup of coffee, smoked another cigarette, and listened with interest while Lord Murchison went on with his story.

≡◇≡◇≡

The next day I arrived at Lady Alroy's house in Park Lane at quarter to five. Her servant opened the door to me.

'I am afraid Lady Alroy has just gone out,' he said.

I went to my club feeling disappointed and unhappy. It was all very strange. In the end I wrote a letter and asked her when I could visit again.

A number of days later I got a strange note from her.

> Park Lane
>
> Dear Lord Murchison,
>   I will be here on Sunday at four o'clock. Please visit me then.
>
>   Yours,
>   Lady Alroy
>
> P.S. Don't write to me here again. I will explain why when I see you.

On Sunday I went to visit Lady Alroy at her house in Park Lane and she was most charming, but when I was leaving she said to me, 'If you want to write to me again, please don't use my real address. Put your letter in another envelope and send it to "Mrs Knox at The Library, Green Street". I can't **receive** letters in this house, don't ask me why.'

In the next few months I saw a lot of Lady Alroy, and there was always a mystery about her. Sometimes I thought that there was another man in her life, but I wasn't sure. One minute I thought that I understood her, and the next minute I knew that I didn't. In the end I decided to ask her to marry me. I was tired of meeting her in secret. I wrote to her at the library.

> Lady Alroy,
> Can I see you next Monday at six o'clock?
> Lord Murchison

She agreed to meet me, and I felt so happy. I thought that I loved her for herself, but I see now that I loved her because of her mystery. And then one day I found out what that mystery was. Or I think that I did.

On the Monday I went to lunch at my uncle's house and I wanted to go to Piccadilly after lunch. I walked the short way there through some very poor and dirty little streets. Suddenly I saw Lady Alroy in front of me. She was wearing a big hat with a heavy **veil**, and was walking very fast. When she arrived at the last house in the street she went up the **steps**, took a key from her bag, opened the front door and went in.

'Here is her mystery!' I thought, and I looked carefully at the house. It had lots of rooms to **rent** in it. On the top step I saw her **handkerchief**.

'She's dropped this,' I said to myself, and put it in my pocket. Then, being a gentleman and not a detective, I went to my club. At six o'clock I visited Lady Alroy's house in Park Lane. When I went in she was lying on a **sofa** wearing a beautiful silver dress with moonstones on it.

receive to get something that somebody sends to you

veil something that a woman puts over her head and face

step a stone stair in front of a house

rent to give money every month for somewhere to live

handkerchief you cry into this

sofa a long soft seat for people to sit on together

'You dropped this
in Cumnor Street
this afternoon.'

'How nice to see you,' she said. 'I have been here all day.'

I pulled the handkerchief out of my pocket and gave it to her.

'You dropped this in Cumnor Street this afternoon,' I said.

She looked at me, afraid, but didn't say a thing.

'What were you doing there?' I asked.

'Don't ask me!' she said, hiding her face in her hands.

'You must tell me. I came here to ask you to be my wife!'

She looked up and said, 'Lord Murchison, there is nothing to tell.'

'You went there to meet someone!' I cried. 'That is your mystery.'

She turned terribly white and said, 'No, I did not.'

'Tell me the truth!' I shouted.

'I am being truthful,' she replied

I was angry and said some terrible things to her. In the end I ran from the house and went away with my friend Alan Colville to Norway. After a month I came back to London and the first thing I saw in the *Morning Post* was the death of Lady Alroy.

LADY ALROY DIES

After catching a bad cold at the theatre five days ago, Lady Alroy died yesterday morning in her house in Park Lane.

I shut myself in my rooms and saw no one.

⸻

'And then you went to the house in Cumnor Street,' I said.

'Yes,' he replied. 'I knocked at the door and a friendly old woman opened it. "Do you have any rooms to rent?" I asked. "Well, there was a lady who was renting the rooms on the ground floor, but I haven't seen her for weeks." she answered. I showed her Lady Alroy's photograph. "That's her!" she said, "And when is she coming back?" "She is dead," I explained. "Oh no," cried the woman, "She was my best **lodger**. She paid three pounds a week just to sit in my **sitting room** sometimes." "Did she meet anyone here?" I asked. "No," said the woman. "She came alone and saw nobody. She just sat here and read books, and sometimes had tea." What could I say? I gave the old woman a pound and went home. But what do you think? I find it so hard to explain. Was she telling the truth or not?'

'I think that she was,' I replied. 'I feel sure that Lady Alroy was a woman who loved mystery. She rented those rooms because she liked going there with a veil over her face, dreaming that she was someone in a book. She loved mystery, but I'm afraid to say that she herself was a **sphinx** without a secret.'

Lord Murchison looked down at the photograph in his hand.

'Yes. Perhaps you're right,' he said at last.

lodger a person who pays to live in another person's house

sitting room a room in a house where people sit and talk

sphinx a monster with a lion's body, a bird's wings and a woman's head; people often think that they are full of mystery

53

READING CHECK

Put these sentences in the correct order. Number them 1–9.

a ☐ Lady Alroy dies.

b ☐ Lady Alroy sends a strange note to Lord Murchison.

c ☐ Lord Murchison follows Lady Alroy and she drops a handkerchief.

d ☐ Lord Murchison visits Lady Alroy's house but she isn't there.

e ☐ Lord Murchison returns the handkerchief to Lady Alroy.

f ☐ Lord Murchison goes to the house in Cumnor Street and talks to an old woman.

g ☐ Lady Alroy asks Lord Murchison to send her letters at a different address.

h ☐ Lord Murchison goes to Norway.

i ☐ Lord Murchison and Lady Alroy have a terrible argument.

WORD WORK

Find words in the flowers to complete Lord Murchison's diary on page 55.

receiveveilrenthandkerchief
sofastepslodgersittingroomsphinx

I knew that Lady Alroy couldn't (a) ....receive.... letters in Park Lane so I went to visit her. I walked up the (b) .... and knocked on the door. She opened it with a strange smile on her face. She looked like an Egyptian (c) .... hiding a terrible secret. I went into the (d) .... after her and we sat down on the (e) .... to talk. I look a small white (f) .... from my pocket and gave it to her.

'This belongs to you,' I said.

'Where did you find it?' she asked.

'Outside a house in Cumnor Street. You were there earlier wearing a (g) .... to hide your face.'

'A house in Cumnor Street?' she said.

'Yes, perhaps you know someone who is a (h) .... there? Or perhaps you (i) .... rooms there yourself so that you can meet your friends there in secret, far from Park Lane.'

GUESS WHAT

What does Lord Murchison do after the story ends? Tick the boxes.

a ☐ He rents the room in Cumnor Street and sits in it thinking about Lady Alroy.

b ☐ He pays a detective to find out more about Lady Alroy.

c ☐ He stays in France and forgets all about Lady Alroy.

d ☐ He marries.

e ☐ He never marries and dies an old and unhappy man.

PROJECT A — *Writing a summary*

1 Read this summary of *Lord Arthur Savile's Crime*.
Cross out five sentences that do not help the summary.

> <u>Lord Arthur Savile's Crime</u>
> 'Lord Arthur Savile's Crime' is a short story by Oscar Wilde. I think
> I've heard of him before. The main characters in the story are Lord
> Arthur Savile, a rich young man, and Mr Podgers, a palmist. I don't
> really believe in palmists, but this story is about one of them. Other
> characters are Sybil (Lord Arthur's girlfriend), Lady Clem (Lord
> Arthur's cousin), and the Dean of Chichester (Lord Arthur's uncle).
> My uncle is a businessman. The story is set mainly in London
> but there are some scenes in Italy too. The story begins when Mr
> Podgers sees murder in Lord Arthur's hand. The plot is about how
> Lord Arthur feels that he must murder someone before he is free to
> marry Sybil. It took me a long time to read it. It is a humorous story
> with a surprise 'twist' at the end. The ending surprised me, at least.

2 Complete the information table for *The Model Millionaire*.

Story title	_____
Author	_____
Main characters	_____
Other characters	_____
Setting	_____
How does story begin?	_____
Plot	_____
Kind of story	_____
Ending	_____

3 Complete this summary using the information in the table on page 56.

'The Model Millionaire' is a _____ by _____ .
The main characters in the story are _____ , a poor young
man, and _____ , a millionaire in beggar's clothes. Other
characters are Hughie's girlfriend, _____ , and his painter
friend, _____ .The story is set mainly in _____
studio and in _____ club. The story begins when
_____ gives _____ to _____ in
_____ studio. The plot is about how _____ can
get the money he needs to _____ . It is a
humorous story with a surprise 'twist' at the end.

4 Complete the table for _The Sphinx without a Secret_.

Story title	The Sphinx without a Secret _____
Author	_____
Main characters	_____
Other characters	_____
Setting	_____
How does story begin?	_____
	_____
Plot	_____
	_____
Kind of story	_____
Ending	_____
	_____

5 Write a summary of _The Sphinx without a Secret_.

PROJECT B   *Story themes*

1 **What are the themes of *Lord Arthur Savile's Crime*? Match them with the sentences from the story.**

Themes

a Wonderful and terrible things often go together in life.

b We often hurt people that we should be nice to.

c Quiet people are often the most dangerous.

d When you believe in something, you can make it happen.

e In everyone good there is something bad and in everyone bad there is something good.

Sentences from the story

1 ☐ Lord Arthur really thinks that Mr Podgers sees murder in his hand, so he decides to become a murderer.

2 ☐ Lord Arthur is planning his murders at the same time as he is thinking of marrying Sybil.

3 ☐ Lord Arthur tries to kill his cousin and his uncle.

4 ☐ Lord Arthur doesn't want to hurt Lady Clem when he kills her.

5 ☐ Lord Arthur doesn't tell his mother or Sybil about what Mr Podgers said.

2 **Oscar Wilde also wrote plays, poems, a novel, and some fairy stories. Match four of these themes with his different works on page 59.**

a It's good to help people who are poorer than you.

b Empty people often want to live interesting lives like someone in a book.

c In everyone good there is something bad, and in everyone bad there is something good.

d Strangers are often more interesting than people that you know really well.

e You cannot know the inside of a person from looking at the outside.

f We often hurt people that we should be nice to.

1 ☐ his poem *The Ballad of Reading Gaol* – about someone who kills the woman he loves.

2 ☐ his comedy play *The Importance of Being Earnest* – about a man who behaves badly in town and well in the country.

3 ☐ his novel *The Picture of Dorian Gray* – about a young man who does terrible things, but who stays young while a picture of his face grows old.

4 ☐ his fairy story *The Happy Prince* – about the statue of a prince who was happy in life but is now sad and tries to help poor people.

3 **What are the themes of the last two stories in this book? Use some of the themes above or some different ideas.**

a *The Model Millionaire*

One theme is: ....

....

How we see this in the story: ....

....

Another theme is: ....

....

How we see this in the story: ....

....

b *The Sphinx without a Secret*

One theme is: ....

....

How we see this in the story: ....

....

Another theme is: ....

....

How we see this in the story: ....

....

4 Can you think of the themes of some different stories?
Write about them like the stories in Activity 3.

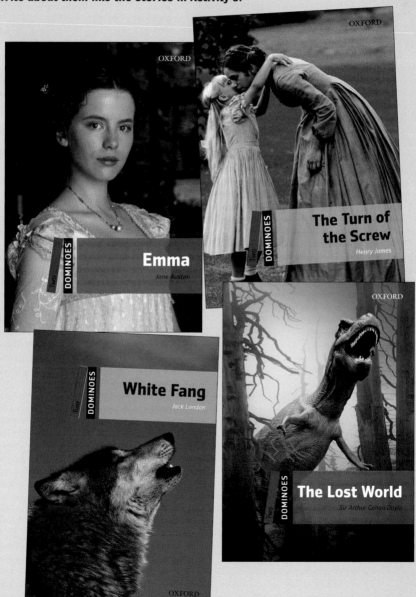

GRAMMAR CHECK

> **Past Simple: affirmative**
>
> With regular verbs we usually add –d/–ed to the infinitive without *to*.
>
> *Oscar Wilde lived at the end of the 19th century. He worked as a writer and editor.*
>
> With regular verbs that end in consonant + –y we change y to i and add –ed.
>
> *study – He studied at Oxford.*
>
> Some verbs are irregular. You must learn their past forms.
>
> *write – He wrote poems, plays, a novel and a lot of children's stories.*

1 Complete the text about Wilde with the Past Simple form of the verbs in brackets.

Wilde's full name a) .....**was**.... (be) Oscar Fingal O'Flahertie Wills Wilde. His parents, Sir William Wilde and Lady Jane Francesca Wilde, b)............... (live) in Dublin. Oscar c)............... (study) at the Portora Royal School at Enniskillen as a boy. He d)............... (win) a place to study at Trinity College, Dublin. After that he e)............... (go) to Oxford to study Latin and Ancient Greek. He f)............... (do) very well. After he g)............... (finish) at Oxford, he h)............... (move) in with a painter friend of his, Frank Miles, in a house in London. His first book of poems i)............... (come) out in 1881. Soon after that he j)............... (visit) America. He k)............... (give) talks there on the study of beautiful things for nearly a year. Then he l)............... (sail) back home to England.

In 1884 Wilde m)...............(marry) Constance Lloyd. They n)............... (have) two children – two boys – Cyril and Vyvyan. From 1887 to 1889, Wilde o)............... (work) as the editor of *Woman's World* magazine. He p)............... (write) most of his best work from 1889 to 1895. Oscar Wilde q)............... (die) in Paris in 1900.

GRAMMAR CHECK

Question tags

We use question tags to check information, or to have a conversation.

It's a story by Oscar Wilde, isn't it?

The tag contains subject + main verb, or auxiliary verb to match the sentence.

He wrote plays too, didn't he?

The Importance of being Ernest is by him, isn't it?

When the sentence is affirmative, the tag is negative.

You've been to a palmist, haven't you?

When the sentence is negative, the tag is affirmative.

You don't believe in palmists, do you?

2 Complete the sentences with the question tags in the box.

are they	aren't they	does he	doesn't he
has he	hasn't he	is he	~~isn't he~~

a Mr Podgers is short and fat, ___isn't he___ ?

b He hasn't got a lot of hair, ...?

c He isn't a manicurist, ...?

d He has green eyes, ...?

e He sees the future in people's hands, ...?

f His offices aren't in East Moon Street, ...?

g His office hours are from ten to four, ...?

h He doesn't see his death in the Thames before it happens, ...?

Mr Podgers

3 Complete the sentences with question tags.

a Lady Windermere has got blue eyes, ___hasn't she___ ?

b Her hair is rich gold in colour, ...?

c She isn't fifty years old, ...?

d She has had three husbands, ...?

e She hasn't got any children, ...?

f She can't live without her palmist, ...?

Lady Windermere

GRAMMAR CHECK

Direct and reported speech

In direct speech we give the words that people say.	In reported speech we put the verb one step into the past and change the pronouns and possessive adjectives.
'Mr Podgers looks at my hand twice a week,' said Lady Windermere.	Lady Windermere said that Mr Podgers looked at her hand twice a week.
'I'll go and find Mr Podgers,' said Lord Arthur.	Lord Arthur said that he would go and find Mr Podgers.

We change personal pronouns and possessive adjectives in reported speech to match the speaker and the situation, too.

4 Rewrite these direct speech sentences as reported speech.

a 'I'm not afraid,' said Lord Arthur.

...... Lord Arthur said that he wasn't afraid. ......

b 'It is the hand of a fine young man,' said Mr Podgers.

....

c 'I'll pay you a hundred pounds,' said Lord Arthur to Mr Podgers.

....

d 'The poison is for my large old Norwegian dog,' said Lord Arthur.

....

e 'I'm ill all the time,' said Lady Clem.

....

f 'There's a yellow sweet inside the box,' said Sybil.

....

g 'I want a bomb,' said Lord Arthur.

....

h 'The police won't get the address from me,' said Lord Arthur.

....

i 'I can get you a clock bomb with no trouble,' said Mr Winckelkopf to Lord Arthur.

....

j 'My wedding dress isn't ready,' said Sybil.

....

GRAMMAR CHECK

Relative clauses with who, which, and that

We can give information about a person or a thing in a relative clause. Relative clauses start with who for a person, which for a thing, and that for a person or a thing.

Hot chocolate is the morning drink which/that arrives for Lord Arthur.

Princess Sophia is the party guest who/that laughs the loudest.

The sentences above are not complete without the information starting with *which/who/that*, so there is no comma.

Bentinck House, which is Lady Windermere's London home, is a good place for parties.

Lord Arthur goes to see Mr Pestle, who has a chemist's shop in Saint James's Street.

The information starting with *which/who* is extra – the sentences above are complete without it – so it comes between commas in the middle of the sentence, or after a comma at the end.

5 Complete these sentences with *who, which,* or *that*.

  a Sybil Merton is the young woman ....who.... loves Lord Arthur.

  b Mr Podgers, ... has offices in West Moon Street, is a palmist.

  c Septimus, ... means 'seventh son' in Latin, is Mr Podger's first name.

  d Lord Arthur lives in Belgrave Square, ... is a very good address in London.

  e Aconitine is the poison .... sounds the best to Lord Arthur.

  f Lord Arthur buys a silver box .... looks very nice for the poison pill.

  g Lady Clem lives in Curzon Street, ... is not far from Piccadilly.

  h The Dean of Chichester, ... is Lord Arthur's uncle, loves clocks.

  i Lord Arthur visits Bayle's Court, ... is near Greek Street in Soho.

  j Count Rouvaloff is the Russian revolutionary .... lives in Bloomsbury.

  k Mr Winckelkopf is the German revolutionary .... sells a bomb to Lord Arthur.

  l Jane Percy, ... writes to Lord Arthur's mother, is the Dean's daughter.

GRAMMAR CHECK

Past Continuous and Past Simple with while and when

We use the Past Continuous for a longer activity in the past, and the Past Simple for a shorter action that happens in the middle of that first activity.

Hughie was visiting the artist Alan Trevor when he met Baron Hausberg.

The word while often goes before the Past Continuous verb and when before the Past Simple verb.

While Trevor was speaking to his frame-maker, Hughie gave the Baron a pound.

When Hughie married Laura, Trevor was standing at his friend's side.

6 Complete these sentences with the Past Continuous or Past Simple form of the verbs in brackets.

a While Hughie __was going__ (go) to visit Laura one day, he __visited__ (visit) his friend Alan Trevor.

b When Hughie .... (arrive), Trevor .... (paint) a picture of an old beggar.

c The old model .... (sit) in the corner of the room when Hughie .... (look) over there.

d While Hughie and Trevor .... (talk), a servant .... (come) into the room.

e Hughie .... (put) his hands in his pockets for some money while the old man .... (move) his arms and legs.

f While Hughie .... (tell) Laura about it all later, she .... (be) angry with him.

g While Trevor .... (finish) his painting of the beggar, the old model .... (ask) him lots of questions about Hughie.

h Trevor and Hughie .... (speak) at their club when Hughie .... (learn) that the old beggar model was really a millionaire.

i Hughie .... (eat) his breakfast the next day when Mr Naudin .... (call) to see him.

j Mr Naudin .... (smile) when he .... (give) Hughie a cheque for £10,000.

GRAMMAR CHECK

Present Perfect

We use the Present Perfect to talk about things happening at some time in the past without saying when.

- ❓ *Have you worked in a bank? Yes, I have/No, I haven't.*
- ➕ *I've worked in a bank.*
- ➖ *I haven't worked as an artist.*

7 Complete the interview with verbs in the Present Perfect.

Interviewer: So, Mr Erskine, what jobs
a) ...*have you done* (you / do) up to now?

Hughie: Well, b)................. (I / work) in a
bank. c)................. (I / try) selling tea. And
d)................. (I / sell) wine, too.

Interviewer: I see. And e)................. (you /
work) as an artist's model?

Hughie: No, f)................. (I / not). But
g)................. (I / know) some interesting
artists and models in my time.

Interviewer: Right. h)................. (you /
meet) Baron Hausberg, the millionaire?

Hughie: Yes, i)................. (I). He's a very
nice man.

Interviewer: j)................. (you and your
wife / see) his houses all over the world?

HUGHIE ERSKINE

Hughie: No, k)................. (we / not). But l)................. (we / visit) him in his
house in London and m)................. (we / eat) from gold plates at his dinner table,
too.

Interviewer: Really?

Hughie: Yes n)................. (we). o)................. (The Baron / be) very good to
my wife and me.